Interactive Rides

by Grace Hansen

AMUSEMENT PARK RIDES

Abdo Kids Jumbo is an Imprint of Abdo Kids
abdopublishing.com

abdopublishing.com

Published by Abdo Kids, a division of ABDO, P.O. Box 398166, Minneapolis, Minnesota 55439.
Copyright © 2019 by Abdo Consulting Group, Inc. International copyrights reserved in all countries.
No part of this book may be reproduced in any form without written permission from the publisher.
Abdo Kids Jumbo™ is a trademark and logo of Abdo Kids.

052018

092018

THIS BOOK CONTAINS
RECYCLED MATERIALS

Photo Credits: Alamy, AP Images, Getty Images, iStock

Production Contributors: Teddy Borth, Jennie Forsberg, Grace Hansen

Design Contributors: Dorothy Toth, Laura Mitchell

Library of Congress Control Number: 2017960578

Publisher's Cataloging-in-Publication Data

Names: Hansen, Grace, author.

Title: Interactive rides / by Grace Hansen.

Description: Minneapolis, Minnesota : Abdo Kids, 2019. | Series: Amusement park rides |
    Includes glossary, index and online resources (page 24).

Identifiers: ISBN 9781532108037 (lib.bdg.) | ISBN 9781532109010 (ebook) |
    ISBN 9781532109508 (Read-to-me ebook)

Subjects: LCSH: Interactive multimedia--Juvenile literature. | Amusement rides--Juvenile literature. |
    Amusement parks--Juvenile literature.

Classification: DDC 791.068--dc23

Table of Contents

Early Dark Rides

Interactive rides are dark rides. Dark rides began to appear in the late 1800s. They were not interactive yet, but they were fun!

Some dark rides, like an old

mill or tunnel of love, were

on water. Riders sat in boats.

Ghost trains were scary

versions of dark rides!

9

It's a Small World is a well-known dark ride. It first opened in 1964 at the New York **World's Fair**. Walt Disney designed it.

11

Going Interactive

Interactive dark rides began to open in the late 1990s. These rides often involve shooting at targets. Riders sit in moving vehicles.

The technology for the ride is complex. The vehicles, the game, and the effects must work together.

Interactive dark rides also have a plot. The plot gives players a goal. In Buzz Lightyear Astro Blasters, riders have to defeat Zurg!

16

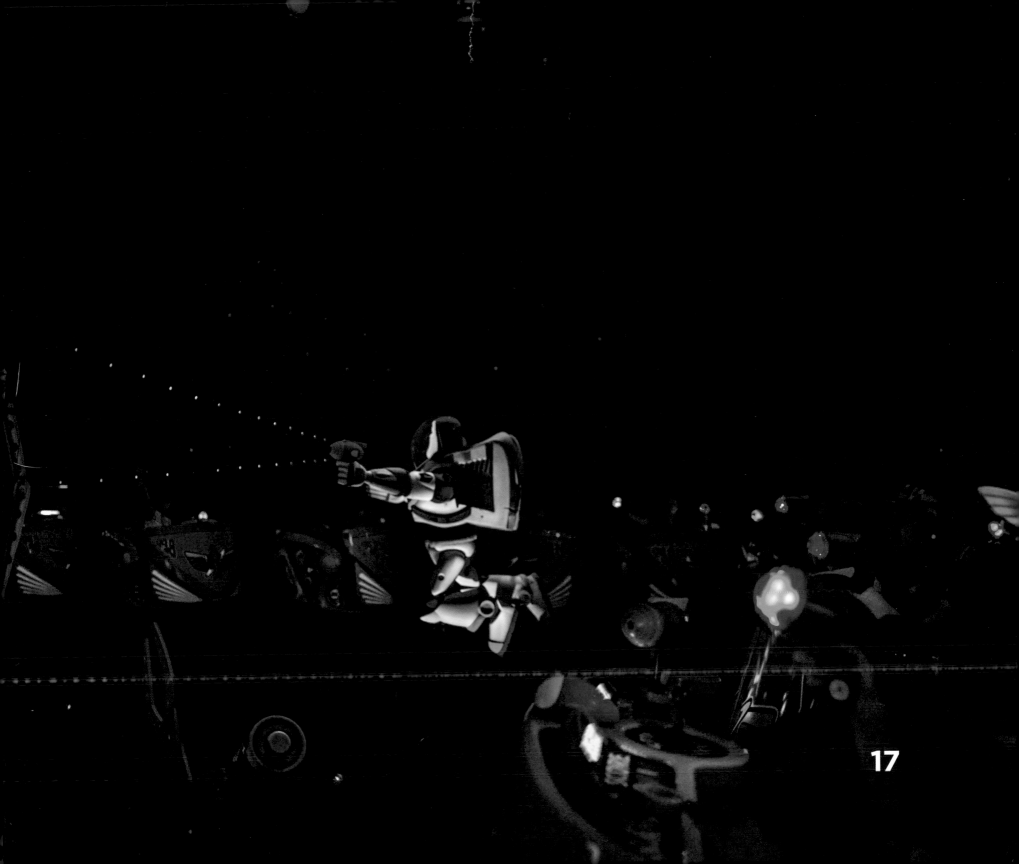

4D and 5D

Disney's Toy Story Mania! opened in 2008. It is a 4D **interactive** dark ride. It cost $80 million to build!

Ghostbusters 5D opened in Germany in 2017. The ghost-hunting car takes 8 people on an exciting adventure!

More Facts

- The Haunted School **interactive** ride at Etnaland asks riders multiple choice questions. Riders are given a grade at the end of the ride.

- Wonder Mountain's Guardian is in Canada. It is an interactive dark ride. But it is also a roller coaster!

- There are three Toy Story Midway Mania! rides in Disney parks. They are in California, Florida, and Tokyo, Japan.

Glossary

interactive – allowing two-way communication between
a computer and a person.

plot – the story line or order of events.

world's fair – an international exhibition that showcases
the industrial, scientific, technological, and artistic creations
of the participating nations.

Index

Abdo Kids ONLINE
FREE! ONLINE MULTIMEDIA RESOURCES

Visit **abdokids.com** and use this code to access crafts, games, videos, and more!

Abdo Kids Code:
AIK8037